Colo's Story

The Life of One Grand Gorilla

By Nancy Roe Pimm

Foreword by Jack Hanna

This publication has been made possible through the generous funding of the
Frances J. Coultrap Endowment at the Columbus Zoo and Aquarium.

This book is dedicated to my mom, Fran Roe-Bono,
a former librarian, for instilling in me her love of books.

—NRP

Text copyright © 2011 by Nancy Roe Pimm
Cover photos copyright © Columbus Zoo and Aquarium

Pimm, Nancy Roe.
  Colo's story : the life of one grand gorilla / by Nancy Roe Pimm ; foreword by Jack Hanna.

  p. : ill. ; cm. -- (The Columbus Zoo books for young readers)

  "This publication has been made possible through the generous funding of the
Frances J. Coultrap Endowment at the Columbus Zoo and Aquarium."
  Summary: Celebrates and chronicles the surprise birth and endearing milestones
of Colo, a gorilla born in 1956 at the Columbus Zoo and Aquarium in Ohio. Follows
Colo's journey from a cuddly baby, to a feisty toddler, to a mother of three, to the
matriarch of one very large gorilla family and now the oldest living gorilla in the world.
  ISBN: 978-0-9841554-4-6 (hardcover)
  ISBN: 978-0-9841554-5-3 (pbk.)
  ISBN: 978-0-9841554-6-0 (ebook)

  1. Colo (Gorilla)--Juvenile literature. 2. Gorilla--Development--
Juvenile literature. 3. Gorilla--Juvenile literature. 4. Captive mammals--
Development--Juvenile literature. 5. Columbus Zoo--Juvenile literature.
6. Colo (Gorilla) 7. Gorilla--Development. 8. Gorilla. 9. Captive
mammals--Development. 10. Columbus Zoo. I. Hanna, Jack, 1947- II. Title.

QL706.2 .P56 2010
599.884

Published by Columbus
Zoological Park Association
9990 Riverside Drive
Powell, OH 43065
www.columbuszoo.org
www.columbuszoobooks.org

Produced for the Columbus
Zoological Park Association by
School Street Media
info@schoolstreetmedia.com
www.schoolstreetmedia.com
Designed by Tracie Maye

Printed in the United States of America

2 4 6 8 10 9 7 5 3 1

Contents

Gorillas have fascinated us for years. To be sure, early African explorers must have been overwhelmed and terrified when they first encountered such impressive creatures in the forests. They must have thought, "The huge silverback males could surely tear a person apart if they had the notion, and they're so fast you could never get away!" Those perceptions of gorillas spread and culminated with the 1933 film, *King Kong*.

When the Columbus Zoo received its first gorillas in the early 1950s, the animals were still perceived as dangerous creatures that should not be housed together. (It wasn't until the studies by George Schaller and the famous Dian Fossey that we learned that gorillas were actually very mellow and family-oriented.) I've noticed the same on my many expeditions to the Virunga Mountains in Rwanda—an adult silverback male quietly lying amongst the lush, green foliage, allowing a baby gorilla to climb all over him and pull at his thick, black hair; mothers feeding infants; and others peacefully making their nighttime nests.

In the early days, the Columbus Zoo staff was proud to have gorillas, even though they weren't kept in a breeding group. Astonishingly, though, the zoo had a big surprise on a late-December day in 1956 when the keepers found a baby gorilla had been born. Not only was that surprising (given the separate housing parameters of the gorillas), but it also was exciting, because this was the first recorded birth of a gorilla in a zoological park—anywhere in the world! The fragile baby was named "Colo," and, as they say, the rest is history.

As it turns out, Colo was the beginning of a magnificent gorilla-breeding program at the Columbus Zoo. Colo had three babies of her own and grandbaby after grandbaby. Her family grew and grew. In 1983, twin gorillas were born at the Columbus Zoo—the first recorded birth of gorilla twins in the western hemisphere. The zoo became well known for its expertise in propagating gorillas and, moreover, for integrating them into family groups.

The staff has even developed a unique surrogate-mother program. Now the Columbus Zoo is proud to have one of the grandest gorilla family trees in the world—and Colo is at the heart of it all.

Of course, there's much more to this story. You'll discover what led to Colo's historic birth, and you'll find out more about her extended family in the following chapters of *Colo's Story: The Life of One Grand Gorilla*.

—*Jack Hanna*
Director Emeritus of the Columbus Zoo and Aquarium

Jack & Suzi Hanna
with twins

Jack with a young mountain gorilla,
Parc des Vulcans, Rwanda

The "Back Story"

Colo's story doesn't really begin on the cold December day when she was born. Like most, hers has a "back story," a story about the events, people, and animals that opened the way for her arrival. That story begins in the jungles of Africa, where two gorillas, one male and one female, were captured and brought to the U.S. They eventually ended up at a relatively unknown little zoo in Ohio.

The Columbus Zoo started out with only six acres of land that housed seven reindeer. Editor Arthur C. Johnson and publisher H. P. Wolfe of *The Columbus Dispatch*, the city's newspaper, had purchased seven Alaskan reindeer for a Christmas celebration. They gave the reindeer to the City of Columbus, agreeing to pay for and build a corral for the reindeer if the city would provide the land and give care, shelter, food, and veterinary attention to the animals. On October 4, 1927, the deal was sealed, and the date marked the beginning of the Columbus Zoo. The zoo added a small number of animals over the next few years, but began to take off in the 1940s.

Monkey Island

By the 1950s, the Columbus Zoo was rated the fastest-growing zoo in the United States; its animal population had almost tripled in only ten years. In 1951, the City of Columbus created a zoo division and took over full operation of the zoo, which had grown to twenty-one acres. In the same year, the city acquired seventy-two acres from the Stanberry Estate. With the help of generous donations and a building fund, the Columbus Zoo began a growth explosion, adding a bird house, a reptile house, a giraffe building, an elephant house, an animal hospital, and an aquarium. According to then-Superintendent Earl Davis, ". . . the grounds and buildings value over $1,000,000, and the collection of mammals, birds, and reptiles [are] close to $200,000."[1] Kiddie Land, made up of several rides and a petting area, was also completed. In 1956 the zoo finished the pedestrian tunnel (it runs under State Route 257) and built a new entrance. But the entrance that made worldwide news was the birth of Colo. The Great Ape House was completed just in time for her arrival.

Over the years, Colo and the Columbus Zoo have grown up together. Colo's celebrity brought fame to the zoo and its gorilla-rearing program. "We know a lot more about gorillas today than we did then, and much of that knowledge can be attributed to the experiences we had with Colo," said Louis DiSabato, zoo director from 1961–1963. "We documented everything."[2]

It has been more than fifty years since Colo surprised the world with her arrival. She remains the queen of the great apes at the zoo. "Colo is the last to accept new people in the gorilla department," says former head keeper Debbie Elder, "but once she has accepted you, you know you have arrived."[3]

Through the years Colo has taught us much about herself and gorillas in general. She taught us that gorillas have emotional as well as physical needs. Gorillas will respect us if we respect them. And, just like people, gorillas thrive in diversified family groups where the young learn from the old and the old from the young.

Now the oldest gorilla in human care and possibly the world, Colo has a lifelong story to share. You'll discover how this grand gorilla has helped make the world a better place for gorillas in zoos and in the wild.

CHAPTER ONE

Gorillas Discover Columbus

Ohio is a long way from Africa. So how did William Presley Said, a young man from a small town near Columbus, Ohio, earn the nickname "Gorilla Bill"?

During the Great Depression, most ten-year-olds in Bexley, Ohio, made their money delivering newspapers. Instead, Bill Said hunted pheasants and rabbits with a 12-gauge shotgun and set traps for muskrats, foxes, raccoons, and skunks. Before finishing grade school, he had earned two hundred dollars selling muskrat pelts.

In 1948, at age twenty-two, Bill traveled to the jungles of Africa to follow his dream of becoming a big-game hunter. One night while sitting around a campfire, he heard other hunters talk about capturing, and not killing, wild animals. The hunters explained to Bill that to make a lot of money, he would need to track down one animal in particular. It was big game, ferocious game, mighty game— the gorilla.

In the 1940s and 1950s, people thought gorillas were man-eating beasts and only the bravest men would dare to hunt them.

French Equatorial Africa was made up of these four present-day countries: Gabon, Republic of the Congo, Central African Republic, and Chad.

Bill was hunting in French Equatorial Africa. The French government protected gorillas from big-game sportsmen, but it allowed collectors like Bill Said to get permits once they showed evidence that the gorillas would be used for scientific studies.

Returning to Africa to capture a gorilla would be expensive. Once he was back in the U.S., Bill needed to find someone to finance his gorilla expedition. He learned the University of Wisconsin was willing to pay, in advance, two thousand dollars for expenses and then another two thousand dollars for each live gorilla that was brought back. According to Jeff Lyttle, author of *Gorillas in Our Midst: The Story of the Columbus Zoo Gorillas*, Bill's permit application stated the university wanted the animals for scientific and psychological experiments.[4]

In the early summer of 1950, Bill Said returned to Africa with a hunting party. For months the hunters battled disease and poor living conditions and didn't once see a gorilla. Bill found a local group of people, the Bacola, who knew the land of the Congo better than anyone. In addition, they were excellent hunters. When Bill asked for their help, the Bacola chief agreed— with one condition. He wanted the "blood of the white gorilla hunter."[5] To prove his commitment to the hunt, Bill held out his arm. The chief used a large hunting knife to make a ten-inch cut. Satisfied with the hunter's dedication, the Bacola tribe helped Bill capture nine young gorillas. That's how the man from Bexley, Ohio, became known as "Gorilla Bill."

The Columbus Zoo Comes Through

Bill and the gorillas left Africa for their journey to the U.S. During the trip, one of the female gorillas froze to death. Bill and eight surviving gorillas landed in New York on December 22, 1950. Soon after landing, Gorilla Bill discovered that the university could no longer afford the gorilla experiments and had no interest in purchasing his animals. Now what was he going to do with eight gorillas?

Thinking fast, Bill called his friend Earl Davis, the superintendent of the Columbus Zoo. "Earl," said the hunter, "I'm stuck here with eight baby gorillas, and this weather is bad. They'll die if I can't unload them soon. Can you help me?"[6] Mr. Davis agreed to try.

Davis called fellow zoo leaders all over the country to help Said find homes for the animals. Out of gratitude, Said sold three of the gorillas to Davis for the sum of ten thousand dollars. The package deal included a male gorilla that was about five years old, another male about eighteen months old, and a female gorilla about twenty-one months old. As a result of this purchase, the Columbus Zoo suddenly had one of the largest gorilla populations in the world. These were the 58th, 59th, and the 60th gorillas in the U.S.

Mac and Millie

Once the gorillas settled into their new environment at the Columbus Zoo, a "name the gorilla" contest was announced. The contest winners were awarded gold-plated lifetime memberships to the Columbus Zoo. The winning entry for the older male was Baron Macombo, named for his birthplace in Macombo, Africa. The female was named Millie Christina (for Earl Davis' wife, Millie), and the younger male became Christopher, for Christopher Columbus. The gorillas' caretakers soon nicknamed them Mac, Millie, and Jimmy.

The public was curious to see these "fearsome" creatures up close, and thousands of them flocked to the zoo to see the star attractions. In 1953, nearly half a million people visited the tiny zoo just north of Columbus, in Powell, Ohio. Although the popularity of the gorillas was apparent, Davis found it difficult to house three gorillas. He decided to trade Christopher (Jimmy) to another zoo. Because gorillas were so rare and valuable, the zoos traded one gorilla for two rhinoceroses and two cheetahs.

Why Zoos "Trade" Animals

In the 50s, 60s, and 70s, zoos operated independently of each other and traded animals among themselves. No organization existed at that time to help coordinate or plan which animal went where and why. All that changed in 1981 when the Association of Zoos and Aquariums (AZA) developed the Species Survival Plan, also known as SSP, to help manage the animal populations in zoos.

As its name suggests, the Species Survival Plan works to help threatened or endangered populations survive. The SSP helps maintain healthy zoo populations and keeps them balanced. A panel of experts, including a chairperson and a studbook keeper, evaluates the needs of the animals and the zoos, which allows the SSP to help coordinate the trades. The studbook keeper watches over and records each animal's pedigree, which traces it back to its wild-born ancestors. Each animal's record includes its birth date, gender, name or names, transfers, parents, and death dates. This is done for all threatened or endangered species found in a zoo.

Many things are considered before making a gorilla transfer. First, how much space a zoo has will determine how many gorillas it should have. Next, the SSP evaluates the animal's records to help decide where it should go. Usually a zoo curator tells the SSP what his or her zoo's needs are. The information is logged into computers, and the SSP makes its animal-exchange recommendations. The final decisions are made among the SSP and the zoos involved.

Today, endangered species are no longer bought and sold, and "ownership" is no longer an issue. The Columbus Zoo and Aquarium houses more than a dozen gorillas, but the zoo owns fewer than a third of them. The others are "on loan" from other zoos, thanks to the SSP, AZA, and the commitment by member zoos to work together to save the species.

Bridgette

Oscar

For example, in 1981, a female gorilla named Bridgette was loaned to the Columbus Zoo from the Henry Doorly Zoo in Omaha, Nebraska, after her mate Casey had died from heart problems. The Columbus Zoo had plenty of room, and Colo's son, Oscar, was in need of a mate. Bridgette came to the Columbus Zoo, and the two proved to be a great match. Oscar and Bridgette had twins, Mosuba and Macombo II, in 1983, and a single male, Motuba, in 1985.

A Secret and a Surprise

Earl Davis put his two gorillas, now called Millie and Mac, in the same habitat in hopes they would breed and reproduce. When Mac acted aggressively toward Millie, Davis decided to separate the gorillas for their safety. Warren Dean Thomas, a twenty-five-year-old veterinary student who worked at the zoo, had a different idea. Before leaving the zoo in the evenings, Thomas put Millie and Mac in the same area, and when he arrived in the mornings, he returned them to their separate habitats. Forty years after the incident, Thomas said, "I was a brash young kid. The arrogance of youth clouded my thinking. When I knew the time was right, another keeper and I quietly started slipping them together, either early in the morning, or at night, before we went home."[7]

Soon Thomas noticed changes in Millie's temperament. She began to show some symptoms of pregnancy, such as weight gain and swollen feet and ankles. When Thomas realized Millie was pregnant, he confessed his disobedience to Earl Davis. Luckily for the young vet student, Davis was thrilled. The superintendent knew this was big news. If all went well, the Columbus Zoo would have what so many other zoos had been striving for—to have the first zoo-born gorilla in the world.

After all the excitement, Thomas and Davis had to figure out when the baby might actually arrive. No one was really sure about how long a gorilla pregnancy, or gestation period, was. There had never been a pregnant gorilla in a zoo, and studies on the subject had never been conducted on gorillas in the wild. The two men guessed it would take nine months, the same it takes for a woman to carry and give birth to a human baby. Based on that, they set an estimated due date to be January 8, 1957.

Mac

Millie

15

CHAPTER TWO

The Tiny Celebrity

On the Saturday before Christmas, December 22, 1956, exactly six years to the day when Bill Said arrived in the U.S. with his eight gorillas, Warren Dean Thomas was making his early morning rounds at the Great Ape House at the Columbus Zoo. He had promised to meet zookeeper, Terry Strawser, for coffee at the Reptile House after feeding the gorillas. When Thomas placed Millie's breakfast of vegetables and hard-boiled eggs into her area, she remained on the platform (about four feet above the floor), where she usually rested and slept. The gorilla loved her mealtimes, but on this day, she looked away, uninterested in her food.

Concerned about her odd behavior, Thomas checked on Millie again around 8:30 A.M. She was still in her rest area, unmoving. Twenty minutes later, before leaving to join his friend for coffee, Thomas checked on Millie one last time. The gorilla seemed to be dazed, her eyes glassy. When Thomas looked down at her untouched food, he saw something that hadn't been there before: a baby gorilla, still in its amniotic sac, lying on the cold, concrete floor.

Thomas and Strawser rescue the newborn gorilla.

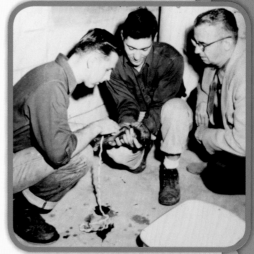

Thomas and Strawser prepare to cut the infant's umbilical cord.

The veterinary student knew he had to act fast. "Without thinking of anything but the baby, I dropped the door on her nest and walked into the cage. I could tell it was alive because I could see it moving."[8]

Holding the fragile bundle in his arms, Thomas raced into the kitchen area of the Great Ape House and removed her from the sac. He swabbed the mucous from her mouth and throat and tried to stimulate breathing by thumping her on the back. The newborn struggled with each breath. "She caught her breath, then lost it," Thomas said. "I knew the strongest stimulant for respiration is carbon dioxide, and the only place I had any was in my own body, so I breathed into her mouth."[9]

The fragile bundle sleeps in a box of clean rags.

Wondering why his friend hadn't shown up for coffee yet, Terry Strawser went to the Great Ape House to look for Thomas. He peered through the window of the locked door and was shocked to find Thomas giving mouth-to-mouth resuscitation to a newborn gorilla. Strawser banged on the door to get his friend's attention. Thomas looked up, but he knew he couldn't leave the baby, even for a few seconds.

He signaled Strawser to get help and continued giving the newborn the rescue breaths. "I was all alone," Thomas recalled. "I knew history was in the making, but I didn't have time to think of anything but keeping the baby alive. In about fifteen minutes the baby was breathing."[10] Strawser returned with a pair of scissors and a hemostat, an instrument used for clamping, and the umbilical cord was cut. The gorilla baby's life had been saved.

The news spread by word of mouth and by telephone throughout the zoo. Stephen Kelley, the zoo's curator of mammals, raced to his car, got a camera out of the trunk, and hurried back to photograph the wet, crying newborn. Earl Davis and his wife rushed in. "I went right away," said Mrs. Davis. "But I was so disappointed! She was a horrible-looking sight. All skin and bones, wrinkled and brown, with a tiny wizened face and pipe-stem arms and legs all covered with coarse black hair. She did have beautiful eyes, though—big and dark."[11]

The baby gorilla spent her first day in a cardboard box filled with clean rags in the boiler room of the Great Ape House, where the boiler and a single lightbulb provided warmth.

the newborn

big, dark eyes

The tiny gorilla
rests at the end of
her first day.

A New Addition: Now What?

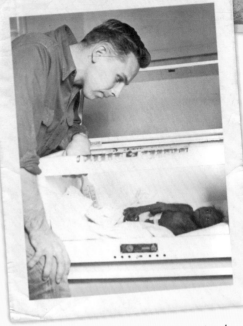

Thomas watches the baby in her incubator.

After all the backslapping, telephone calling, and telegraph sending, no one really knew how to care for a tiny gorilla. Millie, the baby's mother, acted frightened by the birthing experience and appeared to have no maternal instincts. The zoo staff knew they would need to care for and feed the newborn. They wondered: What do you feed a baby gorilla? Could it live on the same baby formula human babies drank? Louis DiSabato, a former curator of mammals at the zoo, explained, "We were all animal experts, but we were writing the textbook on rearing a baby gorilla. I can remember many times we looked at each other and said, 'What do we do now?'"[12]

Since the Columbus Zoo didn't have a veterinarian who specialized in gorilla babies, the next-best person for the job would be a doctor who specialized in human babies. J. Wallace Huntington, the chairman of the zoo commission, called Dr. John Larcomb, a pediatrician in the Columbus area, and asked a question no one in the world had ever asked before: "A baby gorilla was just born at the zoo. What will we feed it?"[13]

Dr. Larcomb was told that the newborn weighed three pounds, four ounces and was fifteen inches long. Even for a human baby, that was small, so the doctor thought she must have been born prematurely. Just as he would have done with a premature baby in the hospital, Dr. Larcomb recommended feeding her sterilized formula and using hospital-clean handling techniques in order to keep the infant safe from germs.

The baby gorilla was nine hours old when the doctors and staff decided to feed her a diluted mixture of one measure of Olac® baby formula mixed with four ounces of boiled, distilled water. Wearing a face mask and white lab coat, veterinarian Dr. Robert Vespers sat in the boiler room of the Great Ape House and gave the infant her first feeding. Much like a human baby, the gorilla nursed from a bottle every three hours, her spindly arms and legs moving spastically. The staff gave her watered-down formula for an entire day before switching her to full-strength formula.

By nightfall, the doctors and the staff had set up an incubator that had been sent from a nearby hospital and placed the little one inside. Twenty-four hours a day, they kept detailed records on a chart by the incubator. They monitored her heartbeat, respiration, and temperature. They even monitored her food intake and bowel movements.

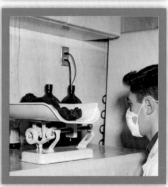

Taking care of baby

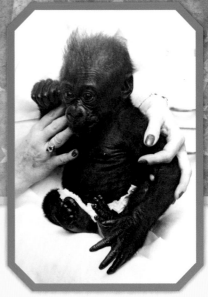

"Sweetie Face"

In 1957, the Columbus Zoo received the first-annual AZA Edward H. Bean award, given for a rare birth of a zoo animal on the North American continent. In addition, Dr. Ernst M. Lang from Basel, Switzerland, said of Colo's birth: "super-exceptional event of utmost importance in the study of gorillas." (*Columbus Citizen Journal*, December 26, 1956)

Christmas came three days early for the Columbus Zoo. In a matter of hours, the zoo went from being an obscure place that wasn't even considered among the top zoos in the state of Ohio to making headlines worldwide. Hours after the historic birth, the producers of *The Today Show* called. The mayor of Columbus, M. E. Sensenbrenner, passed out cigars with bands that read, "It's a Girl." *The New York Times* began printing daily reports on the progress of the tiny celebrity. The newborn even appeared on the pages of both *Time* and *Life*, two of the nation's most popular magazines. Officials from zoos all over the world either came to visit the baby gorilla or sent her gifts.

Baby Gets a Name

With twenty-four-hour-a-day observation and the love and care of five attendants, the tiny gorilla thrived over the next days and weeks. People started calling her "Cuddles" and "Sweetie Face." She gurgled, sucked her thumb, and played with, and at times sucked, her toes. She lifted her head while lying on her back. Just before feeding time, she made little squeaking noises and hungrily smacked her lips. "She looks better to me every feeding," Thomas said. "During her last feeding, she grabbed my shirt, and I tested her strength. She could hold her own weight with one hand."[14]

In the baby gorilla's seventh week, the staff added soup, cereal, vegetables, vitamins, fruit, and a little meat to her diet. Her favorite food was applesauce, but she didn't like peas or spinach much. As one keeper noted, "Peas in any combination would bring out the gorilla in her."[15] In two and a half months, she grew from three pounds, four ounces to seven pounds, eight ounces.

The newborn celebrity made headlines in the city's morning newspaper, *The Columbus-Citizen Journal*, on a regular basis. With the zoo's approval, the newspaper held a contest to name the baby gorilla. The newspaper's staff offered to pay the winner twenty-five dollars, and the zoo's commissioner, J. Wallace Huntington, offered to match it with twenty-five dollars of his own money. When Ohio native and movie star Clark Gable heard the news, he offered a one-hundred-dollar bond to the winner, making the grand total $150 (a nice sum in 1956).

Within a month of the gorilla's birth, a name was chosen from the 7,500 entries. Some of the choices included: Wrinkles, Victoria, Star, Babs, ColumBess, Peanuts, and Zuzu. Mrs. Howard Brannon of Zanesville, Ohio, sent in the winning name, which she came up with by combining the words "Columbus" and "Ohio." The little gorilla girl was named Colo.

Name the baby gorilla!

CHAPTER THREE

Colo's Early Years

All the attention and good medical care gave the once-fragile baby what she needed to grow stronger, more active, and more confident. After Colo's fourth day in the incubator, Earl Davis said, "When she's on her tummy, she moves all over the incubator and tears up her bed. We're going to have to make a bigger incubator."[16]

After fifteen weeks in the incubator, feisty Colo wanted out! She banged on the sides of the glass incubator with her teething ring and loosened the light bulb that hung over her head. Instead of building a bigger incubator, Davis asked the Columbus City Council for $11,000 in emergency funds to build the little star a nursery. Following much debate, the funds were approved.

After receiving the money, an 18' x 25' addition was constructed onto the Great Ape House. No longer in an incubator, Colo was free to roam around her new nursery. Anyone who entered the nursery had to wear a mask and a white nurse uniform or lab coat. A stove, a sink, and a refrigerator were in a corner of the nursery for food storage, preparation, and clean up. Heat radiated around the lower edges of the room to keep the floors warm. Floor-to-ceiling glass on two sides allowed Colo's fans to do plenty of gorilla gazing. And gaze they did. More than one million people visited the zoo in 1957, shattering the zoo's previous attendance records.

From Tickles to Tantrums

Colo was treated like a human baby. She had daily Ivory-soap baths and baby-oil rubdowns. Everyday she wore an outfit from her wardrobe of baby clothes. Every evening she was dressed in her pajamas and tucked into bed. She even had a collection of dress-up clothes for special occasions. She had lots of toys, but Colo usually picked out a rubber monkey and carried it around.

The little diaper-clad gorilla dazzled the zoo's visitors. Caretakers swaddled her in receiving blankets and rocked her. "I took her from the enclosure so we could sleep together," said former zoo curator's wife, Joan Kelley. "She encircled my neck with her little arms, cuddled up under my neck, and that is how we slept on the narrow cot pulled close to her enclosure. On mild evenings in the spring, I wrapped Colo in a receiving blanket and took her for walks around the zoo grounds."[17]

On her first Easter, Colo wore ruffled panties, a pink dress, and a frilly bonnet. Nibbling on a daffodil, she was a sight indeed! She loved to dress up and wear hats.

As a toddler, Colo loved to roll, play, and—ever the silly girl—even stand on her head, all to the amusement of her onlookers. She put food bowls on her head as hats. The keepers gave her piggyback rides. Colo loved to come up behind them and untie their apron strings. One of her favorite tricks was hanging from the ceiling bars of the nursery, like on a jungle gym, and drop down on her unsuspecting attendants.

As she grew in size and spunk, Colo became more difficult to handle. She spit between her teeth with amazing accuracy and made a habit of spitting into the keepers' eyes. She learned to spring the latch in her enclosure and blocked the door when her attendants tried to leave. When she was younger, she had made small, sad, whining sounds when one of her favorite attendants left, but as a toddler, she threw full-out screaming tantrums.

toys & tantrums

"The coddling of Colo ended," said Mrs. Davis, "the night she spread apart the bars at the back of her nursery and toddled down the hall to the kitchen. She threw her hairy arms about the nurse who was giving a bottle to a baby bear and frightened her half to death. It took over an hour to get Colo back to where she belonged. After that, she was caged like the rest of the apes."[18]

A Great Ape Education

She may have been housed like the others, but Colo was not and never would be like the rest of the apes. From the moment of her birth, she was studied by zookeepers and scientists. The husband-and-wife team of Dr. Benjamin Pasamanick, the director of research at the Columbus Psychiatric Hospital, and Dr. Hilda Knoblich, head of pediatric psychology at Columbus Children's Hospital, came for regular visits to study and compare gorilla development with human development. They also tested the theory that a longer a species stays in infancy, dependent on its mother for survival, the more intelligent it will become as an adult. The research team began its work when the infant gorilla was only eighteen days old and continued every two weeks for the next year. Colo was tested in her nursery, and by her first birthday, she had been tested more than twenty times.

The tests revealed that the gorilla reached the infant milestones of sitting, standing, and walking in half the time human babies took to do the same things. Although Colo's motor skills developed twice as fast as human babies', tests on her thinking skills suggested her thought process slowed down at age six months. The researchers believed her quick motor development and stunted thinking ability proved their theory that a short period of infancy leads to a lower level of intellectual development. Disgusted with the researchers and their conclusion, Superintendent Davis said, "We who have been outwitted by Colo time and time again—I wonder where *we'd* rate in the I.Q. test conducted by this team."[19]

finger painting

"I think this is the greatest thing that has ever happened in zoo history. All zoo men in the world had looked forward to this time, and I'm proud it happened in Ohio."

—former Cleveland Zoo Director Fletcher A. Reynolds as quoted in *Columbus Citizen Journal*, December 30, 1956.

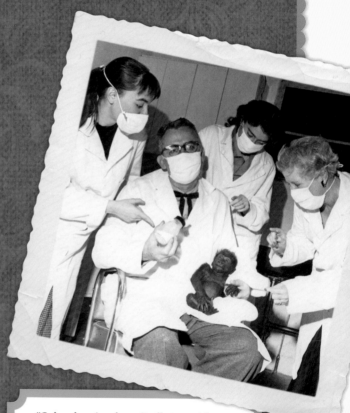

"Columbus is where it all started for gorillas. No matter what happens now or in the future, the zoo will always be remembered for Colo's birth."

—former Columbus Zoo Director Louis DiSabato as quoted in *Gorillas in Our Midst*, page 52.

29

CHAPTER FOUR

Colo and Company

Colo's antics and fits of rage became more and more of a challenge for the zoo staff. She had become too attached and dependent on her human keepers and began acting like a spoiled child. The staff agreed that the best thing for Colo would be to have a playmate—not a human, but another gorilla. By the time Colo was eighteen months old, the zoo had raised enough money to purchase Bongo, a young male gorilla named for the city nearest to the site of his capture in Africa. He arrived at the Columbus Zoo on October 1, 1958. Bongo was thought to be about eighteen months old and weighed nineteen pounds.

After Bongo was given a clean bill of health, the long-awaited day came. Wearing a white dress decorated with pinwheels and triangles, Colo leaped around her habitat at the sight of another gorilla. She climbed the bars and reached out to touch him. Bongo seemed to be more frightened than excited, but he tentatively reached out to Colo. The zoo staff proclaimed the two to be a perfect match.

By March 11, 1959, nursery records showed the pair was sleeping peacefully together. The toddlers had regular play dates, and Bongo gave Colo the balance she needed to have one foot in the human world and one in the gorilla world.

Colo and Bongo: a perfect pair

Welcome, Bongo!

Big Scares and Hard Times

Colo

The Columbus Zoo survived some difficult times in the early 1960s. Tragedy struck when Superintendent Earl Davis, who had run the zoo for sixteen years, died of cancer in December 1960. A few years later, in the spring of 1963, tuberculosis (TB) broke out in the Great Ape House. Colo, Bongo, Mac, Millie, and orangutans Jiggs and Maggie were all contaminated with a human strain of TB, which can infect the lungs and other body parts. On March 8, 1963, headlines in *The Columbus Dispatch* proclaimed, "Colo Death Predicted in 90 Days." According to the article, Dr. Robert Henthorne, a professor of veterinary medicine at The Ohio State University, stated that once a gorilla or larger primate contracts tuberculosis, the life expectancy is ninety days. Dr. James Savoy, zoo director after Davis's death, was advised by The Ohio State University veterinarians to shoot all the infected primates before the disease spread to more animals. "Because of Colo," Dr. Savoy said, "I couldn't do it."[20]

After talking with doctors from the Tuberculosis Society of Columbus and Franklin County and veterinarians from the United States Air Force and The Ohio State University, Dr. Savoy directed the keepers to give the sick animals the same medicine used for humans with tuberculosis. The keepers administered the drugs in orange juice to hide the medicine taste. The drugs were effective, and the primate population was saved.

After the scare was over, the medical staff tracked down the source of the infection. One of the keepers had been diagnosed with tuberculosis before the zoo outbreak, so the vets determined that the gorillas had become infected through human contact. Soon after, the Columbus Zoo became the first zoo to put glass between the great apes and onlookers, thus protecting the animals from human germs.

By 1964, only eight years after Colo's birth, the zoo's annual attendance had dropped more than half, from an all-time high of more than one million visitors during Colo's first year to a mere 370,000. Leaders of the zoo formed a committee to look for solutions. Instead, they found problems. The facilities and the animal housing were deteriorating, and shutting down the zoo became an option.

The Columbus community wasn't ready to give up, however. With the financial help of well-known businessman, Daniel Galbreath, and Mayor M. E. Sensenbrenner, many much-needed improvements were made at the zoo. In 1967, voters passed the first bond issue earmarked specifically for the zoo. With that income, improvements to plumbing and animal housing were made possible.

Colo's First Baby

With the health of both the zoo and the primates restored, life for Colo and Bongo returned to normal. The two gorillas shared a 12' x 15' habitat with cement floors and tile walls. Dr. Lee Simmons, assistant superintendent at the zoo from 1963 to 1966, sometimes went into the enclosure and played with the pair. "They would check your pockets and see if you had anything up your shirt sleeve or down your collar. Both of them liked to put their fingers in your mouth, open it up, and check your teeth. Colo was very friendly and socialized with humans, but she was an ornery gal."

When the pair grew older, they became breeding mates. In 1967, a medical test confirmed that Colo was pregnant, and she got a place of her own. On February 2, 1968, Colo gave birth to the first second-generation gorilla born in human care. After cleaning her baby, she picked it up, held the tiny gorilla in front of her nose, and gazed at the infant. Following her inspection, Colo took her four-pound baby girl to Dr. Savoy and the keepers to show her off. "As soon as it was born, it cried. It sounded just like a baby's cry," Dr. Savoy later told reporters. "And with the sure sign of life, I began to click my heels with joy."[21]

Emmy

Colo cuddled the baby and seemed to be a nurturing mother, but she had never watched a mother gorilla care for her young. The keepers paid close attention to see if Colo knew what to do. They waited for three days for her to nurse the baby, but she never did. In order to save the newborn's life, the veterinarian decided it was necessary to move the infant from Colo and raise it in the nursery. After the baby was removed, Colo sat quietly in a corner and appeared depressed for several days. She soon recovered, however, and lived with Bongo once again.

The news of the gorilla baby's birth made headlines because the zoo had set yet another record—this time for the first second-generation gorilla birth in a zoo. As with Colo, a contest was held to name the new baby. The winner was a local ten-year-old who suggested the name Emmy, after the Columbus mayor, M. E. Sensenbrenner. Emmy was two months old when she made her public debut on April 6, 1968.

Two More Stars Are Born

About a year and a half after Emmy's birth, on July 18, 1969, Colo gave birth to a son. The announcement of his birth shared the front page of the July 20th *Columbus Dispatch* with the news of the Apollo 11 moon landing. Weighing only four pounds, twelve ounces, the newborn was soon removed from Colo because of another tuberculosis scare that had just occurred a few months before. The baby went directly into an incubator to be raised in the same nursery where his big sister, Emmy, was. This time, seven-year-old Barbie Bean came up with the baby gorilla's name: Oscar. She wrote, "Because Colo has nothing but winners, her little boy should be named Oscar, to go along with her Emmy."[22]

Oscar

Toní

Colo's third baby, another female, came as complete surprise. On December 28, 1971, former keepers Bill Cupps and Scotty Roy arrived in the early morning to feed the gorillas. Cupps remembers the shock of seeing Colo holding a baby. "Nobody even knew she was pregnant," he said. "She held the baby, but she never fed it." The three-pound, fifteen-ounce baby was soon named Toni, completing the trio of award-winning names.*

*The names came from the top three awards in the entertainment industry: Oscar, for best films; Emmy, for best television programming; and Tony (Toni) for best Broadway plays.

Colo and Bongo

Colo

Toni went to the zoo nursery to be raised with her siblings Emmy, nearly four years old, and Oscar, seventeen months old. All three wore clothes, drank from bottles, and ate baby food, just as their mother had. The only difference was that they had each other for company.

At the time, removing the babies to raise them in a nursery was the best option available. Columbus Zoo Director Emeritus "Jungle" Jack Hanna explains, "The gorillas were so valuable that most zoos did not want to take the chance of the babies dying. What they were doing was destroying the family unit. We didn't know. We learned a lot from Colo."

CHAPTER FIVE

Changes for Colo

When Jack Hanna arrived as zoo director in 1978, he fought to have the gorillas' living area modernized to ease the tension in the Great Ape House. Colo, Bongo, Mac, and Millie were living in small, barred enclosures with bare cement walls and floors. They stayed indoors and never had the opportunity to go outside. In their cramped quarters, they had absolutely nothing to do. Former head keeper Dianna Frisch recalls, "Overall, it was not a pleasant environment. There was always tension in the building that could be felt because of the setup, and the gorillas acted out in frustration."

"It didn't seem right to me," Jack Hanna explains when asked about those years. "We had this world-famous gorilla collection, and I had to find a way to make it more natural."

In 1979, the former Elephant House was renovated to house the gorilla family, and it had both inside housing and an outdoor recreation area. Frisch says, "Jack understood the need for gorillas to be in a family group. He also knew that they needed to be out of doors, and he was willing to listen to the keepers who felt strongly that they could make changes to give the gorillas happier and more productive lives."

The New Great Ape House

37

a new outdoor habitat

Bongo

When the renovations were completed, the gorillas' enclosures had a door that opened to a grassy yard with a tree and a shallow, concrete pool. Bongo moved first and stepped to the door. He squinted, brushed the grass with his knuckles, and quickly backed up. Tentatively, he felt the grass one more time and backed up again. Finally, Bongo sprinted out the door— with Colo following close behind. For the first time in their adult lives, Colo and Bongo breathed in the open air and felt the warmth of sunshine.

Colo Day

When Colo turned twenty-five in 1981, Mayor Tom Moody declared a "Colo Day." Colo celebrated her big day by eating a whole-wheat cake. The Columbus Zoo and Aquarium is the only zoo in the world to house four generations of zoo-born gorillas.

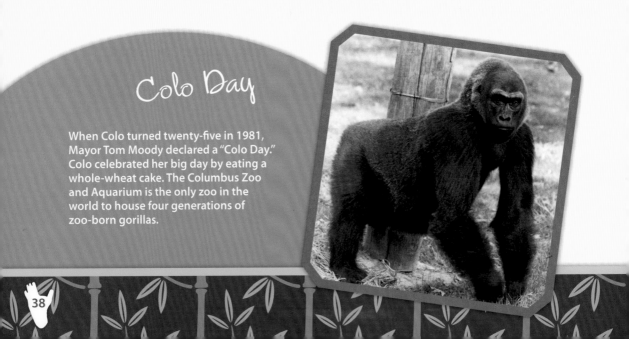

Grandma Colo

Another big change came in 1979. Colo became a grandmother. Daughter Toni gave birth to a female baby, Cora, which stood for Columbus Ohio Rare Ape. Although the staff was hopeful Toni could care for her young one, she seemed to be unaware of how to do that. Gorilla keeper Barbara Jones says, "The main reason the mother gorillas failed to care for their young is because, beginning with Colo, they were not raised by their own mothers, and they had no examples." For Cora's safety and survival, she was taken from her mother to be raised in the nursery, but was returned to her gorilla family when she was three years old.

Grandma Colo

In 1983, Colo became a grandmother again, and this time the staff was in for another surprise. Colo's son Oscar and his wild-born mate Bridgette became the parents of twin boys, Mosuba and Macombo II—the first set of gorilla twins born in the western hemisphere. Although they were raised in the nursery, these babies benefited from some of the big changes that were being made in the ways zoos cared for their gorilla populations.

twins Mosuba and Macombo II

39

Dian Fossey, a famous gorilla expert, had visited the Columbus Zoo while promoting her book and movie, *Gorillas in the Mist*. Fossey had spent sixteen years living among the mountain gorillas in Africa, and she shared her knowledge of gorillas with the staff at the Columbus Zoo. She explained that wild gorillas forage for food all day, and at night they build nests to sleep in. She stressed the need for groups to be made up of gorillas of all different ages and of allowing mother gorillas to rear their own infants. She explained that when gorillas are kept in social groups, they learn from one another. The animals are meant to live in closely bonded family groups where habits and knowledge can be handed down from one gorilla generation to the next. The Columbus Zoo was eager to make the changes needed so its gorillas would benefit from hanging out with each other.

The gorillas got a brand-new environment as a result of all the staff had learned from Dian Fossey. Finished in 1985, the Gorilla Villa habitat had mesh sides, trees, grass, hanging ropes, and lots of open space where the gorillas could romp, play, and forage for food.

© The Dian Fossey Gorilla Fund International

Dian Fossey & the Gorilla Villa

Colo's Growing Family

A silverback named Mumbah headed Colo's family group. A silverback is an older male, usually more than twelve years old, and he leads and protects the family. The group also had two females, Bathsheba and Lulu; Colo's eight-year-old granddaughter, Cora; and her grandtwins, Mosuba and Macombo II. After they were all together in their new habitat, Colo showed an interest in mothering the twins, caring for them as if they were her own. She made sure the twins ate, and she taught them how to defend themselves and make gorilla noises.

In 1986, Bongo and Bridgette mated, and she gave birth to a son, Fossey. For the first time in Columbus Zoo history, a baby gorilla was left in the habitat to be raised by his gorilla mom and dad. Everyone was hopeful that when Colo's daughter, Toni, gave birth to her fourth infant a year later, she'd be able to care for it herself. The new baby, a male, arrived on "Jungle" Jack Hanna's fortieth birthday, so he was named J.J. Unfortunately, Toni still showed no interest in caring for her baby. J.J. had to be raised in the nursery, but with one noteworthy change: he wore diapers but never wore clothes and was taken to see gorillas daily.

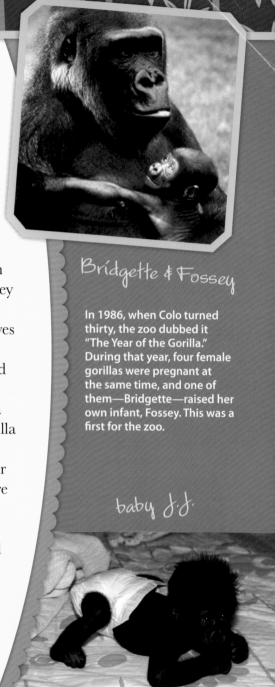

Bridgette & Fossey

In 1986, when Colo turned thirty, the zoo dubbed it "The Year of the Gorilla." During that year, four female gorillas were pregnant at the same time, and one of them—Bridgette—raised her own infant, Fossey. This was a first for the zoo.

baby J.J.

After a year in the nursery, the keepers wanted to place J.J. in an adopted gorilla family as soon as possible. Because of Colo's interest in mothering the twins for the previous couple of years, she was chosen to be J.J.'s surrogate, or substitute, mom. For a while, Colo was taken from her group to live side-by-side with fourteen-month-old J.J. They lived in two separate rooms divided by only a wire screen. Some days the gorillas sat alongside each other; other days they touched each other through the mesh.

One day J.J. reached through the screen and took some of Colo's food, and Colo didn't seem at all upset by it. Since gorillas only share with you if they like you, this was a great sign. The keepers knew it was finally time to open the door between Colo and J.J. Colo stood in the doorway. J.J. moved to within two feet of her and stopped. He looked up, walked to Colo, and reached around to climb on her back, just as he would have done with his own gorilla mother. Colo had never had *anything* on her back, but she bent down to help him up. The keepers are misty-eyed as they recall the story. "When Colo lifted J.J. up and put him on her back, it was incredible," says conservationist and former keeper Charlene Jendry. The keepers were deeply touched to witness J.J. climbing onto Colo's back. "It was a lovely gift," says former head keeper Beth Armstrong.

surrogate mom, Colo, with J.J.

At the age of thirty-one, Colo became the first surrogate gorilla mother at the Columbus Zoo, despite never having had her own mother to teach her. After having three offspring of her own and then becoming the grandmother to fifteen others, Colo finally had the opportunity to mother a baby.

Once Colo and J.J. established their bond, they were put back in the family group. Colo shared her meals of fruits and vegetables with J.J. She snuggled him all through the night. But most of all, Colo made sure no harm came to her grandson, especially from the four-year-old twins who had earned the reputation of being "rude boys." The twins were full of energy. If one wasn't getting into trouble, the other one was.

One day the twins began to play tug-of-war, using J.J. as the rope. Colo went after one of the twins. She held him down and put her mouth around him without biting down. Beth Armstrong witnessed that event, too. "It scared the bejesus out of them," she recalls. "They learned not to mess with J.J. They knew Colo would come to his aid." After that lesson, whenever Colo was watching, the twins treated J.J. like a prince. Soon, the three gorillas romped, tickled, played, chased, and rolled around. Among the staff, J.J. became known as the "third twin."

the "rude boys"—twins Mosuba & Macombo II

Jumoke

Muchana

In 1997, Colo's granddaughter Jumoke (Toni's daughter) gave birth to a son, Jontu. The baby was left in the habitat with his gorilla family, making Jumoke—who was raised in the surrogate program—the first zoo-born gorilla to raise her own infant at the Columbus Zoo. Jumoke nursed the baby, but his great-grandma Colo, at age forty-one, became his primary caretaker from the beginning. She kept track of Jontu throughout the day. Although baby gorillas usually ride on their mothers' backs, Jontu chose to ride on Colo's back. Colo protected Jontu from getting hurt and taught him gorilla ways. Jumoke fed her baby and played with him, but Jontu's bond was with Colo. She nurtured her great-grandson, but she also disciplined him when needed. Jontu had the best of both worlds: Jumoke, a fun-loving mom, and Colo, a nurturing great-grandma.

When Jumoke's second son, Muchana, came along three years later, Colo was not interested in raising another little one. She would not let Muchana ride on her back. Forty-four-year-old Colo made it clear that she wanted less and less to do with the rearing of the youngsters. Jumoke had learned from her grandma Colo and seemed ready to step up and be a full-time mother to Muchana. Colo was content just to be a great-grandmother.

Gorilla Mother Love

When Colo's first grandchild, Cora, was put into the Great Ape House with her gorilla family after having only human contact for her first three years, she screamed for days. Vice President of Animal Care, Dusty Lombardi remembers it well: "It was terrible for Cora. She had never even seen a gorilla before. I was a new keeper following my supervisor's orders, but I knew there had to be a better way. I vowed that this would never happen again. We came up with the idea of raising the babies next to gorillas and having humans act like gorilla moms so the transition would be more natural. We owe a lot to Cora for her courage that day. She was the one that turned the light bulb on for me."

Cora's troubles helped urge the zoo to start a gorilla surrogacy program. Instead of a being kept isolated in the gorilla nursery, the babies are raised in a room near a gorilla family, allowing the youngster to see, smell, and watch the family interact throughout the day. The gorillas are even able to touch or kiss each other through the mesh partition.

Instead of treating a gorilla baby like a human baby, the human keepers behave like gorilla mothers. The keepers pace around the room on all fours with the baby gorilla clinging to their backs. At feeding time, the humans grunt and "share" their food with the infant. After lunch, they roll around with the little one, tickling, laughing, and play biting. When the day is done, the little baby wraps its arms around the neck of the keeper, and they sleep together through the night.

"The most natural thing for a baby gorilla is to be held," says surrogacy program coordinator, Barbara Jones. "It gives them security and confidence." Today, Barbara Jones and Maureen Casale travel throughout the country teaching other zoos the fundamentals of the Columbus Zoo surrogacy program.

These days, fifty-four-year-old Colo lives alone most of the time, but this first surrogate mother still shows an interest in the babies in the surrogacy program. She sits close to the mesh, keeping a watchful eye on the little ones.

CHAPTER SIX

Colo's Golden Years

Beginning in her mid-forties, Colo began to distance herself from the family group, preferring to sit alone. As Muchana and Jontu grew older, they became more physical, and the roughhousing increased within the family group. Every morning when the family left its private sleeping area to go on public display, Colo would hesitate. The keepers noticed her resistance and felt she was trying to let them know that she preferred to live alone, without all the commotion of family life.

Near her fiftieth birthday, Colo chose to live in her own room. Her habitat is close to her family group, so even in her solitude she keeps an eye on the gorillas around her. Colo is the matriarch, or oldest female, of her family, and she still keeps everyone in line. At any sign of a scuffle, Colo runs up and down the glass, coughing or vocalizing, to keep order in her gorilla family. She watches them play and interact, and they are always aware of her presence.

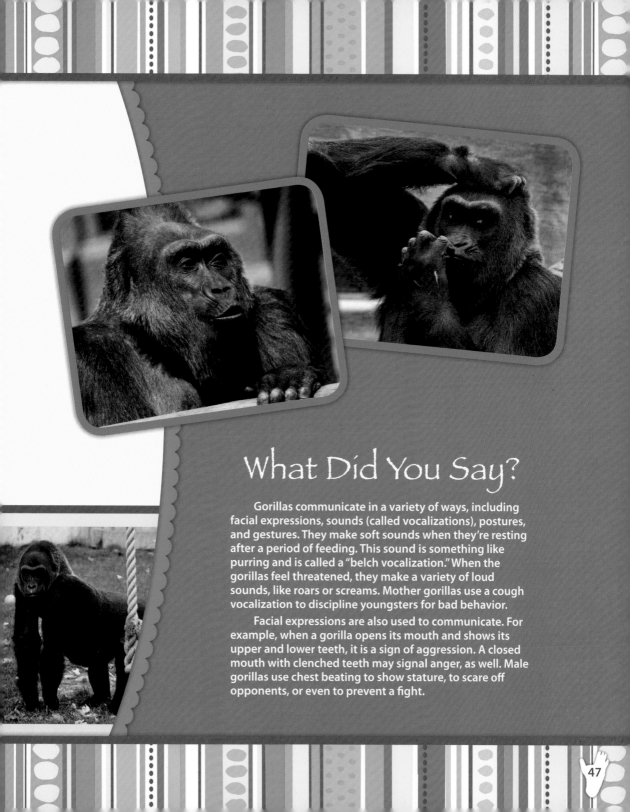

What Did You Say?

Gorillas communicate in a variety of ways, including facial expressions, sounds (called vocalizations), postures, and gestures. They make soft sounds when they're resting after a period of feeding. This sound is something like purring and is called a "belch vocalization." When the gorillas feel threatened, they make a variety of loud sounds, like roars or screams. Mother gorillas use a cough vocalization to discipline youngsters for bad behavior.

Facial expressions are also used to communicate. For example, when a gorilla opens its mouth and shows its upper and lower teeth, it is a sign of aggression. A closed mouth with clenched teeth may signal anger, as well. Male gorillas use chest beating to show stature, to scare off opponents, or even to prevent a fight.

Great Ape Brain Games

In the 1960s the word *enrichment* had not been coined yet in the gorilla world, but it was used in education. The keepers knew that due to the intelligence of the gorillas, they needed activities to stimulate them. The gorillas were given burlap bags, toilet paper, and paper towels to play with. The keepers scattered sunflower seeds and raisins under the hay to make finding food a challenge.

In the late 1980s, the keepers began a more sophisticated enrichment program for the gorillas. The activities gave the great apes an opportunity to show their intelligence, and they were challenged. Food puzzles—plastic pipes filled with peanut butter and raisins—were scattered throughout the habitats. The only way to get to the food was through small holes in the pipe. Branches were left in the habitat, but only one would fit through the hole. "Colo was the first gorilla to figure it out," says former head keeper Dianna Frisch. "She picked it up within minutes. The others watched, and then they all began to do it, but Colo led the way."

Today, more than thirty enrichment items are regularly cycled through to relieve boredom and challenge the gorillas' intellect. Some include trash-can lids, milk crates, barrels, cereal boxes with treats, unbreakable mirrors, register tape, bubbles, finger painting, cardboard tubes with treats, sidewalk chalk, balls, and honey dabbed around the area. They also enjoy music.

Mumba works on a puzzle.

Colo checks out a "birthday box" on her 48th birthday.

The keepers train with the gorillas to establish behaviors that assist in medical procedures, such as monitoring their heart rate and taking their blood pressure and temperature. Debby Ames is one of Colo's trainers. She gets Colo to place her hands in different spots, teaches Colo to push her shoulder to the mesh to receive injections, and has her move her chest close to accommodate a stethoscope. "Colo doesn't always cooperate. She's my toughest customer. One day she actually grabbed the toothbrush out of my hand and brushed her own teeth. She has a way of telling you that you are insulting her," says Ames. "Colo gives you a look as if to say, 'I can do these things myself.'"

hanging out

playtime with J.J. and the twins

A Day in the Life of Colo

At 7:00 A.M., it's lights on. The keepers go from room to room, making sure everyone is accounted for and everything is as they left it the night before. After the building check, breakfast is prepared. Colo begins each day sipping on a cup of herbal tea. According to keeper Jane McEvoy, "Colo prefers to have her tea with a hint of blueberry or raspberry, and if it doesn't pass the sniff test, she regally tilts her chin up and turns her head away."

After her morning tea, Colo is spoon-fed a bowl of pureed fruit and oatmeal, along with some nutritional biscuits. Her mid-morning snack consists of carrots or sweet potatoes and juice. Sometimes she takes a morning nap.

When noon rolls around, the keepers toss her a scattered feeding of iceberg lettuce, popcorn, dry cereal, and other greens. If she spies a hose of running water, she closes her eyes, opens her mouth, purses her lips, and literally begs for a drink. "She is very insistent if she wants a drink from the hose," says McEvoy.

puzzle feeder   relaxing

Colo spends her afternoons engaged in different enrichment exercises that stimulate her mentally and, at times, physically. One of Colo's favorites is a puzzle feeder called the Holtzrugal®, a toy made of recycled plastic with holes drilled in it. Treats are hidden inside, and it takes time and smarts to get the goodies out.

Colo likes to play dress up, too. She wraps rolls of paper (supplied by the keepers) around her neck as if she were wearing a scarf. Some days she wraps it around her waist, making a paper skirt. Colo loves putting almost anything on her head. She wears coconut shells and orange or banana peels, but sometimes she puts straw-colored wood wool on her head like a wig and struts around as a blonde.

Colo ends her day with an evening meal of tomatoes, apples, bananas, nutritional biscuits, and lots of cut-up vegetables, like celery and cucumbers. In the course of a day, she consumes about four to five pounds of fruits and vegetables. Finally, it's time for the room check. All of the gorillas are tucked into their sleeping areas, and at 7:00 P.M. it's lights out.

One Grand Gorilla

Colo has been called many things by those who have come to know and love her. Her nicknames have included Cuddles, Sweetie Face, Princess, Grouch, the Queen Bee, the Grand Mum, and Granny Pants. "I don't think there is anyone who has ever worked with Colo who didn't just fall in love with her," says keeper Jane McEvoy. "We are all at her service, and she loves to outsmart the keepers."

Call her what you want, she's still the boss. Colo lets everyone know what is acceptable and what isn't, and over the years she has earned the utmost respect from her gorilla family and her human family. The keepers agree that it's easy to tell whom Colo likes and doesn't like. Here are a few stories about Colo and her "entourage."

From Target Practice to Trust

Scotty Roy and Bill Cupps worked with the gorillas in the 1970s. Roy had a good relationship with Colo. Cupps, on the other hand, came from the Children's Zoo area and had no experience with gorillas. He quickly became target practice for Colo. She spit on him and threw things at him.

"I'd be washing the windows, and all of a sudden, I would feel something dripping from my hair and down the back of my neck," says Cupps. The public thought it was funny, but by 1976 Cupps had become frustrated by Colo's awful treatment. He asked Roy for advice. Roy gave Cupps some gorilla books and told him to go home and read them. He also told

One smart gorilla!

Cupps that he needed to trust the gorillas in order for them to trust him, especially Colo.

Cupps recalls, "I read the books and took Scotty [Roy]'s advice. One day while I was making my rounds, Colo made a friendly sound to me. I stepped up to the bars. She put her hand out real slow. I thought to myself, 'Okay, this is the day I have to show Colo I trust her.' Her other arm came out, and she put it around my shoulder. It was a scary moment. She gently pulled me into a hug. I talked to her real softly. I asked her to be careful with me. We were face to face. She looked me in the eye, and for a second, I thought she was about to kiss me! All of a sudden, she released me, and I stepped away." Colo and Cupps became really good friends that day.

Dan Nellis began working as a keeper in the Great Ape House in 1992, and he was the first male keeper to work with Colo since Bill Cupps, ten years before. (Cupps left the area in the early- to mid-1980s.) Nellis says, "It's Colo's job to let the keepers know the rules of the Great Ape House. It took a while for her to warm up to me. Before all of the renovations, the Great Ape House was a dark place. Colo would hide, and when I came around the corner, she blasted me in the face with whatever breakfast she had. Her spits were fast and accurate. One day, Charlene Jendry, a conservationist and former keeper, witnessed Colo spitting her breakfast of peas and carrots into my open eyes. Jendry walked up to Colo and said, 'Colo, don't you think he's had enough? You've been spitting on him for two years now.' Colo turned to Jendry and spit in her face. Jendry turned to me and said, 'You're on your own!'"

the queen of the great apes

Colo and the Pony Parade

Near the end of August 2000, Colo spent her days lying around, refusing to eat or drink. Worried about her health, the zoo staff decided to send her to the hospital on the zoo grounds for a diagnosis and treatment. Many tests were run, and the veterinarians discovered she had an inflamed digestive tract. While being treated with antibiotics and undergoing more tests, Colo stayed for ten days in the hospital.

The keepers kept close watch over Colo and tried to give her things to do to relieve her boredom. Then one day, the ponies arrived! The small animals from the zoo's pony rides filed down the hallway on their way to get their yearly physicals. Colo craned her neck to check out the commotion. When the keepers noticed her interest, they continued to march the ponies up and down the hallway to give their patient a pony parade.

The zoo staff agreed that having some "animal company" cheered Colo up. The staff continued to bring the ponies by, and Sweep, the zoo's border collie, also came for regular visits.

Some of the keepers felt that Colo left the hospital a different animal. According to keeper Jane McEvoy: "She likes to interact with her keepers more now. I can tell when I walk in if she is in a playful mood. I'll crouch down and say, 'C'mon, Granny.' Colo will wind up her arm, shuffle across the habitat, bang her shoulder to the mesh, and run up and down with me."

the animal
hospital

Let's Make a Deal, Colo-Style

Colo is a master of the art of negotiation. She loves to trade and haggle for things. Charlene Jendry recalls, "Once, she found a set of plastic keys in her habitat. Colo placed her foot on top of the keys and tried to hide her new treasure from us. Afraid it would be a choking hazard, I tried to barter with her by offering to exchange the keys for some peanuts. Colo gave me a look of bored disinterest and kept her foot on top of the keys. Obviously, it was going to take more than peanuts to get her to surrender the keys!" Jendry rushed to the kitchen and came back with fresh pineapple. After giving it some thought, Colo finally lifted her foot, revealing the hidden keys. She picked them up, opened the ring, and took the keys off one at a time. Using this technique, Colo managed to negotiate not one, but five pieces of fresh pineapple.

Former head keeper Dianna Frisch says of Colo, "She is a unique combination of human intelligence and gorilla intelligence." One day a zoo visitor had thrown a fistful of pennies into her exhibit, which could be a possible choking hazard. Colo collected all of the pennies, cupped them in her hands, and shook them. Dianna brought out a box of Oreo cookies to use for barter. Colo gave one penny for each cookie until she had eaten nine of the tasty treats. "She liked cookies, but when I really had to up the ante, I would get Colo a Wendy's Frosty®. That was the big prize with the gorillas."

Jack Hanna adds, "Colo is a unique animal. She is very, very intelligent. She is methodical. She watches every move you make. Colo looks and thinks first."

"She watches every move you make."

the grand negotiator

Old Friends

One day during the winter of 1998, Warren Dean Thomas stopped by the Columbus Zoo to visit the gorilla he had resuscitated from the cold, concrete floor of the Great Ape House forty-two years earlier. It had been a long time since the two had seen each other, and head keeper Audra Meinelt was fascinated by Colo's reaction to him. Meinelt says, "Although Colo is a sociable animal, she does not seek out extra attention from the keeper staff the way some of the other gorillas do. When Warren Thomas came to visit, Colo was at the back of her room, leaning against the doors. She began moving her lips as if she was blowing kisses to him. When he came over and knelt down, she went over to him, reached out a finger, and stroked his head. This was a softer side of Colo that I was not used to seeing."

the softer side of Colo

Colo's Health and Heart

Colo is the oldest gorilla living in a zoological park. Despite her age, her only medical problem is arthritis. Monthly medication keeps her limber, and the keepers have installed platforms in her habitat to make it easier for her to get around. However, in 2009, Colo had a health scare that alarmed a lot of people. She had been acting depressed and lethargic, and there were worries that it may be her heart.

Former Columbus Zoo Director Jeff Swanagan called Jack Hanna to say he thought Colo might not survive the night. That day the grandchildren of the famous Von Trapp family were in town visiting the Hannas. Swanagan asked Jack if the Von Trapps would come to the zoo to sing a song for Colo. When the family sang "Amazing Grace" acappella, Colo lifted her head and listened. "It was the most amazing sight I've ever seen," said Jack. "I'm not saying it saved her life. I'm just saying the next day she was more active."

It was time for Colo to get a thorough exam, especially to check for heart problems.

Colo Turns Fifty!

On December 22, 2006, *Good Morning America* aired a segment about Colo's fiftieth birthday, so the entire country could be a part of the celebration.

Crowds gathered at the zoo to sing to this grand gorilla and watch her dive into her sugar-free carrot cake. Throughout the week, Columbus Zoo and Aquarium visitors wrote well wishes and birthday greetings on a "gorilla-sized" birthday card.

Doing this kind of checkup on a "senior" gorilla had some risks. She would have to be anesthetized for the exam. According to Dr. Joseph Donovan, an anesthesiologist who worked with the zoo, in "people years" Colo was like an eighty- or ninety-year-old human. As any family would, the zoo staff worried about what the doctors would find and how Colo would endure the exam itself. The other doctors involved included the zoo's veterinarian, Dr. Michael Barrie, and cardiologist, Peter George. Dr. George usually worked on people, but he explained, "We look for the same thing we're looking for in a human heart. If you showed someone her heart, they'd confuse it with a human heart. It's kind of surreal."

During the three-hour procedure, the doctors did a full medical workup on Colo, checking for any signs of disease so they could treat or manage whatever they found. They took blood samples for testing, gave Colo her vaccinations, examined her teeth, and took x-rays. Dr. George used an ultrasound to see Colo's heart. At the end of the day, there was good news. Colo was remarkably healthy for a fifty-two-year-old gorilla. She had an infection, which was treated with antibiotics, and she made a full recovery.

"She's the Columbus Zoo icon," said Dr. Donovan, "and she seems to keep on keepin' on."

Caring for Aging Gorillas

Getting older isn't any easier if you're a gorilla. The great apes have many of the same problems humans have when they are "up in years." They deal with arthritis, bad teeth, irritation with younger gorilla behavior, and, for the females, menopause. Some older gorillas have even received hip replacements. Often the same treatment used for humans has been effective for gorillas. Says Dr. Pam Dennis, a veterinarian at Cleveland Metroparks Zoo and The Ohio State University, "For so long, human treatment has been based on experiments with animals. Now, we're treating animals with humans as medical models."

A Living Legacy

When Warren Dean Thomas found a newborn gorilla barely alive on the floor of her mother's habitat at the Columbus Zoo more than five decades ago, no one really understood the profound influence this tiny baby would have. The Columbus Zoo hadn't even really planned to have gorillas in the first place, let alone start a world-class breeding program. When Colo was born, no one was prepared to care for and raise a gorilla baby.

Yet, against all odds, the tiny baby thrived, becoming the first zoo-born gorilla in the world. At the time, no one knew how Colo's life would change the way we look at gorillas, both in zoos and in the wild. Millions of people worldwide were fascinated to watch Colo grow up; over the years, hundreds of animal experts learned how to care for and protect these family-centered animals.

one grand gorilla

Colo is the grand matriarch of a large family: she's had three children, nineteen grandchildren (including gorilla twins), five great-grandchildren, and two great-great grandchildren. Beyond Colo's own family, gorillas the world over have benefited from her life because "Colo's story" helped raise awareness of dangers the great apes face, dangers that could lead to the extinction of their species. We can hope that Colo's legacy will be that such an extinction never happens.

CHAPTER EIGHT

Gorilla Conservation:
Protecting Colo's Cousins in the Wild

Along with the privilege of having wild animals at a zoo comes the responsibility to help their cousins in the wild. This responsibility increases as species become endangered. "One of the strengths of zoos is giving the visitors the opportunity to make the connection between wild-born animals and zoo animals. It's a circle of communication," says conservationist Rebecca Rose. "When visitors come through our zoo and have the opportunity to meet a gorilla like Colo, hopefully there will be an emotional connection that will move them to do something. It's an incredible opportunity to raise awareness."

Mbeli Bai Gorilla Project

The Columbus Zoo and Aquarium plays many roles in supporting wildlife conservation. For the western lowland gorillas, like Colo, the zoo supports the Mbeli Bai Gorilla Project in Central Africa's Republic of Congo. *Bai* is an African word for a natural, large, swampy clearing in the forest. Groups of large animals, including the gorilla, go to the bai to congregate and forage the vegetation. Gorillas are known for staying hidden in the dense jungles, so the clearing gives researchers an opportunity to study gorillas out in the open.

By studying the comings and goings of gorillas, researchers have made many important discoveries. The animal scientists study social behaviors and non-vocal communication, and they take DNA fingerprinting. DNA fingerprinting compares sets of DNA samples to determine whether the individuals are related or not. By collecting and tracking the DNA of the gorillas, the researchers learn which silverback has fathered which babies. They also use fingerprinting to count and track gorillas and to discover the evolutionary history of the gorilla. According to Rebecca Rose, "Research is critical to conservation—knowledge is power!" Gorilla researchers have made many significant discoveries. The research is important for education, but it is equally important for conservation.

The scientists not only track the population of the western lowland gorillas, but they also keep a watchful eye on them. "This area was a killing field before this project was set up," said Rose. "Poachers would go to the bai to kill the large animals. But the long-term gorilla project's continuous presence of researchers is one of the best deterrents to poachers that you can have."

The researchers share their findings with the local people and the local government. The natives are showing more of an interest in protecting their wildlife, and the government is creating protected areas for the gorillas. The Mbeli Bai Gorilla Project has started an educational program called Club Ebobo (*ebobo* is "gorilla" in the local language.) Leaders of the club take kids from the local villages to the study sites to teach them about gorillas and their issues.

western lowland
gorilla & baby

Pan African Sanctuary Alliance

Exotic pet trading and bush-meat hunting is illegal, but it's still a growing problem. Adult gorillas are being slaughtered for bush meat, a term for the flesh of wild animals that live in the forested land of Africa known as "the bush." With the killing of the adults, gorilla babies are left as orphans. More and more sanctuaries have sprung up across Africa to care for the orphaned gorillas. Raising orphaned apes is time-consuming and expensive. The Columbus Zoo and Aquarium supports PASA, the Pan African Sanctuary Alliance, which has united eighteen rehabilitation centers or sanctuaries that care for thousands of orphaned chimpanzees, bonobos, gorillas, and other endangered primates across Africa. All great apes are endangered, and the numbers of gorillas, chimpanzees, and bonobos have plummeted. "I think it is a great fit for the zoo to support accredited sanctuaries," says Rebecca Rose. "After all, a zoo is really a sanctuary for animals."

Hunting isn't the only concern. The number-one threat to gorillas in the wild is loss of habitat, and this threat continues with increased logging. Gorillas naturally like to stay hidden among the jungle trees. Logging operations build roads through the dense jungles. Because of the increased logging and deforestation, the apes become exposed to poachers and their population declines.

Another threat to the gorilla population is disease, especially ebola, which has wiped out entire families of gorillas. Ebola is a virus that causes a fever that results in massive internal and external bleeding. It kills within two weeks after the symptoms appear. There is no known cure.

baby gorilla

Partners in Conservation

The Columbus Zoo and Aquarium also supports the conservation and humanitarian efforts of Partners in Conservation (PIC), a group that was founded in 1991 by staff and docent volunteers at the Columbus Zoo. From the beginning, the Columbus Zoo has funded PIC's annual operating budget. PIC's central

mountain gorilla & baby

mission is to help preserve wildlife—including the endangered mountain gorillas—and to economically improve the lives of the people living near the rainforests in Rwanda and the Democratic Republic of Congo (DRC). Some of the natives become involved in illegal bush hunting and/or deforestation to escape poverty. PIC believes that if the needs of the local population are respectfully assisted, the forest will remain intact, and the animals will survive.

The money raised by PIC is used to pay the salaries of veterinarians who care for the mountain gorillas, provide energy-saving stoves that enable the local people to use less wood for cooking and heating purposes, and fund a reforestation project that will plant 80,000 seedlings in the DRC. PIC is also working to educate beekeepers with modern techniques, including smokers that are used to calm the bees while honey is collected. Before the beekeepers had learned of the smokers, they accidentally started forest fires when they burned dry grass to calm the bees. According to Charlene Jendry, a founding member of PIC, "Zoo staff, docents, teachers, and students are working together to improve the lives of people, help save the rain forests, and help protect the wildlife that live there."

Colo's Family Tree

Green: **Male**

Purple: **Female**

*estimated birth year
CZ= Columbus Zoo

Pongi
wild born 1963*

Bridgette
wild born 1961*
d: 7 Oct 1987

Joansie
wild born 1962*
d: 1983

Macombo II
(twin)
CZ born
26 Oct 1983

Mosuba
(twin)
CZ born
26 Oct 1983

Motuba
CZ born
25 Jan 1985

Roscoe
CZ born
31 July 1980
d: 29 July 1981

Oscar/Joansie
(O.J.)
CZ born
31 July 1981

Lang
CZ born
31 Dec 1982
d: 6 Jan 1983

Monifa
CZ born
3 Janc 1998

Colbridge
CZ born
8 Oct 1987
d: 1 May 1994

Mwelu
CZ born
16 July 1986

Casode
CZ born
16 Aug 1993

Mata Hari
CZ born
16 Aug 1974

Hasani
San Francisco Zoo born
8 Dec 2008

Baraka
CZ born
11 Apr 1992

Timu
Cincinnati Zoo born
9 Oct 1995

Samson
CZ born
1 May 1995

Baina
Henry Doorly Zoo born
8 Apr 2005
d: 9 Oct 2008

Bambio*
Henry Doorly Zoo born
16 Aug 2003
*father unknown

Hadari
Henry Doorly Zoo born
27 July 2009

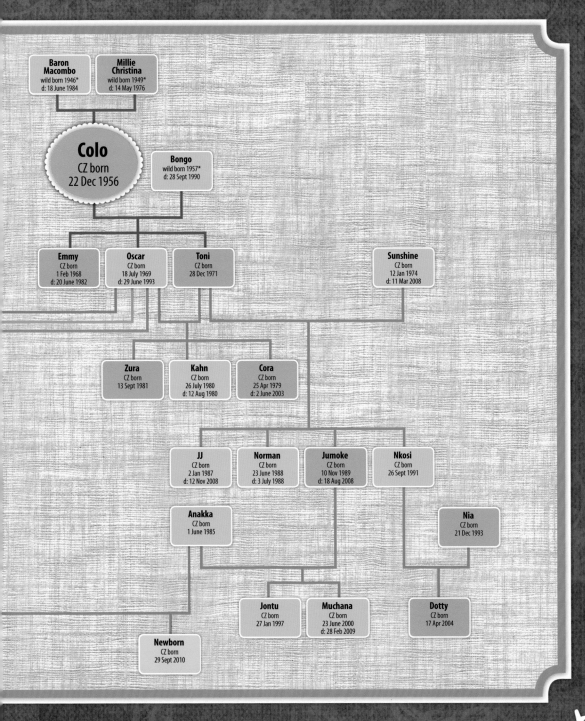

Colo's Family Scrapbook

Bongo

Mumbah

Jumoke

Mosuba

Lulu and baby

Macombo II

Macombo

Bongo, Bridgette, & Fossey

Emmy

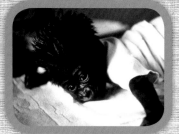

Oscar

Toni

Bridgette & Fossey

Colo

ENDNOTES

[1]"The History of Franklin County: The Columbus Zoo," *The Ohio Historical Review*, page 6.

[2]Jeff Lyttle, *Gorillas in Our Midst*, Columbus, Ohio: The Ohio State University Press, 1997, page 51.

[3]Interview with Debbie Elder, former head keeper for gorillas at the Columbus Zoo and Aquarium, 19 August 2010.

[4]Jeff Lyttle, page 14.

[5]Ibid., page 17.

[6]"Colo," *The Columbus Dispatch*, June 12, 1966.

[7]Jeff Lyttle, page 35.

[8]"Zoo Gorilla Gives Birth," Columbus Citizen Journal[ital title], December 22, 1956.

[9]Ibid.

[10]Ibid.

[11]"Colo," *The Columbus Dispatch*, June 12, 1966.

[12]Jeff Lyttle, page 44.

[13]Freda Koch, "Colo's Counselor: Clintonville Doctor Making Medical History with Care of World's Most Famous Baby," *The [Clintonville] Booster*, March 7, 1957.

[14]"This Gorilla Baby—She's Almost Human," *Columbus Citizen Journal*, December 25, 1956.

[15]"Colo's Counselor," *The Ohio Chronicle*, No. 22, March 16, 1957, page 1.

[16]"Name Baby Gorilla Prize Jumps to $150," *Columbus Citizen Journal*, December 26, 1956.

[17]Interview with Joan Kelley, wife of former Columbus Zoo curator Stephen Kelley, June 17, 2010.

[18]"Colo," *The Columbus Dispatch*, June 12, 1966.

[19]Ibid.

[20]Ibid.

[21]Jeff Lyttle, page 60.

[22]"First Emmy, Now Oscar for Colo," *Zoo Views*, Vol. 1, No. 2, Columbus, Ohio, Fall 1969.

All other quotes are from the interviews found in the Bibliography on page 74.

ACKNOWLEDGMENTS

Thanks to the many people from the Columbus Zoo and Aquarium for their help with my research and for answering so many questions: Vice President of Animal Care, Dusty Lombardi; conservationist Rebecca Rose; Sheila Campbell, librarian of the Columbus Zoo; and intern Tiffany Hill. Thanks to Director of Animal Health, Dr. Michael Barrie, for the interesting animal hospital tour, and to all those who took the time to share their love and knowledge of Colo, including Charlene Jendry, Debbie Elder, Debby Ames, Bill Cupps, Audra Meinelt, Dan Nellis, Jane McEvoy, Dianna Frisch, Barbara Jones, Joan Kelley, Dr. Lee Simmons, and Adele Dodge.

Sincere thanks to Director Emeritus Jack Hanna for taking the time to share some really amazing stories, to Grahm Jones for finding such wonderful photos, and to Fran Bäby for her help in starting the zoo's publishing program.

This book would not be possible without the expertise and guidance from my wonderful editor, Tanya Dean Anderson. I love the way we work together! Thanks for all of the advice from my writing group: Linda Gerber, Margaret Peterson Haddix, Linda Stanek, Jenny Patton, and Erin McClellan, and from my "readers," dear friend Carol Neale and my mom, Fran Roe-Bono.

Finally, to Colo for opening the hearts and minds of so many and making the world a better place for gorillas.

RECOMMENDED READING

Gish, Melissa. *Gorillas*. Living Wild series. Falls Church, VA: Creative Education, 2010.

Hatkoff, Juliana, Isabella, and Craig and Dr. Paula Kahumbu. *Looking for Miza: The True Story of the Mountain Gorilla Family Who Rescued One of Their Own*. New York: Scholastic, 2008.

Kushner, Jill Menkes. *Who on Earth Is Dian Fossey? Defender of the Mountain Gorillas*. Scientists Saving the Earth series. Berkeley Heights, NJ: Enslow Publishers, 2009.

Lewin, Ted and Betsy. *Gorilla Walk*. New York: HarperCollins Publishers, 1999.

Lyttle, Jeff. *Gorillas in Our Midst: The Story of the Columbus Zoo Gorillas*. Columbus, OH: The Ohio State University Press, 1997.

Nichols, Michael and Elizabeth Carney. *Face to Face with Gorillas*. National Geographic Children's Books, 2009.

Orme, Helen. *Gorillas in Danger*. New York: Bearport Publishing, 2007.

Pimm, Nancy Roe. *The Heart of The Beast: Eight Great Gorilla Stories*. Minneapolis, MN: Lerner/Darby Creek Publishing, 2007.

Simon, Seymour. *Gorillas*. New York: HarperCollins/Smithsonian, 2008.

Sobol, Richard. *Breakfast in the Rainforest: A Visit with Mountain Gorillas*. Cambridge, MA: Candlewick Press, 2008.

Taylor, Marianne. *Mountain Gorilla*. Chicago: Heinemann Library, 2004.

Turner, Pamela S. *Gorilla Doctors: Saving Endangered Great Apes*. Scientists in the Field series. Boston: Houghton Mifflin Books for Children, 2005.

BIBLIOGRAPHY

Interviews

Ames, Debby, Keeper at the Columbus Zoo and Aquarium. Interview by author. Powell, Ohio, 9 June 2010.

Barrie, Dr. Michael, DVM. Director of Animal Health at the Columbus Zoo and Aquarium. Interviews by author. Powell, Ohio, 19 June 2010 and 19 August 2010.

Cupps, Bill. Retired Keeper of the Columbus Zoo and Aquarium. Interview by author. Columbus, Ohio, 19 June 2010.

Frisch, Dianna. Former Head Keeper at the Columbus Zoo and Aquarium. Interview by author. Columbus, Ohio, 17 June 2010.

Hanna, Jack. Director Emeritus of the Columbus Zoo and Aquarium. Interview by author. Powell, Ohio, 22 June 2010.

Jendry, Charlene. Conservationist and former gorilla keeper at the Columbus Zoo and Aquarium. Interview by author. Powell, Ohio, 17 June 2010.

Jones, Barbara. Gorilla Keeper at the Columbus Zoo and Aquarium. Interview by author. Powell, Ohio, 16 June 2010.

Kelley, Joan. Caretaker of Colo as an infant. Phone interview by author. Powell, Ohio, 28 May 2010.

McEvoy Jane. Keeper at the Columbus Zoo and Aquarium. Interview by author. Powell, Ohio, 9 June 2010.

Meinelt, Audra. Head Keeper at the Columbus Zoo and Aquarium. Interview by author. Powell, Ohio, 17 June 2010.

Nellis, Dan. Keeper at the Columbus Zoo and Aquarium. Interview by author. Powell, Ohio, 9 June 2010

Rose, Rebecca. Conservationist at the Columbus Zoo and Aquarium. Interview by author. Powell, Ohio, 9 June 2010.

Simmons, Dr. Lee, DVM and former Assistant Superintendent 1963–1966. Interview by author. Powell, Ohio, 22 June 2010.

Books

Lyttle, Jeff. *Gorillas in Our Midst—The Story of the Columbus Zoo Gorillas*. Columbus, OH: Ohio State University Press, 1997.

Articles

Barker, Judith. "Grandma Gorilla." *Highlights for Children*, June 1993.

Chase, Dan. "History of the Columbus Zoo—1927 to 1987," 1987.

"Colo." *The Columbus Dispatch Magazine*, 12 June 1966.

"Colo Death Predicted in 90 Days." *The Columbus Dispatch*, 11 March 1963.

"Colo's Counselor." *The Ohio Chronicle*. No. 22. 16 March 1957.

"Council Ponders 'Renting' Gorilla." *Columbus Citizen Journal*, 18 January 1957.

"First Emmy, Now Oscar For Colo." *Zoo Views*. Powell, Ohio: Columbus Zoo. Vol. 1, No. 2. Fall 1969.

Gray, Kathy Lynn. "Colo to Undergo Risky Heart Tests." *The Columbus Dispatch*, 26 June 2009.

"History of Franklin County, The: The Columbus Zoo." *Ohio Historical Review Periodical*.

Koch, Freda. "Colo's Counselor: Clintonville Doctor Making Medical History with Care of World's Most Famous Baby." *The Booster*, 7 March 1957.

"Offspring of Colo Beginning of Zoo Era." *Beastly Banner*. Powell, Ohio: Columbus Zoo and Aquarium. Vol. 11, Issue 6. November/ December 2001.

Sullivan, Katherine. "Zoo Gorilla Gives Birth." *The Columbus Citizen Journal*, 22 December 1956.

Sullivan, Katherine. "It's A 'Coo' at the Zoo for the Baby Gorilla." *The Columbus Citizen Journal*, 24 December 1956.

Sullivan, Katherine. "This Gorilla Baby—She's Almost Human." *The Columbus Citizen Journal*, 25 December 1956.

Sullivan, Katherine. "Baby Gorilla Worth $50,000, But Who'd Sell?" *The Columbus Citizen Journal*, 17 January 1957.

Sullivan, Katherine. "Name Baby Gorilla Prize Jumps To $150." *The Columbus Citizen Journal*, 26 December 1956.

Switzer, John. "Grandma May Guard Gorilla." *The Columbus Dispatch*, 13 June 1990.

Tullis, Matt. "Primates Beyond Primetime." *The Columbus Dispatch*, 20 April 2007.

Weaver, Don. "Columbus's Zoo Needs a Nursery." *The Columbus Citizen Journal*, 30 December 1956.

PHOTO CREDITS

Mission Statement

We exist to enrich our community's quality of life and to inspire a greater appreciation of wildlife for the advancement of conservation action.

About the Columbus Zoo and Aquarium

Founded in 1927, the Columbus Zoo and Aquarium gained international recognition and stature with the 1956 birth of Colo, the world's first zoo-born gorilla. Today, the zoo is a nationally and internationally acclaimed conservation center, housing more than 700 species, including 37 endangered and threatened species. Annually, the zoo supports more than 70 wildlife conservation projects around the world through its Conservation Fund and Partners in Conservation.

In addition to its role as a global conservation leader, the Columbus Zoo and Aquarium is a renowned year-round education and recreation facility for visitors of all ages, backgrounds, and experiences. Each year, the zoo attracts more than 1.8 million visitors, educates more than 250,000 children and adults, and serves as a field trip destination for more than 130,000 students. The zoo resides on 580 acres, making it one of the fastest-growing zoos in the world and the third-largest municipally affiliated zoo in North America.

The Columbus Zoo and Aquarium is an Association of Zoo and Aquariums (AZA) accredited institution, which requires member organizations to adhere to high standards in animal care and demonstrate strong programs in conservation, research, and education.

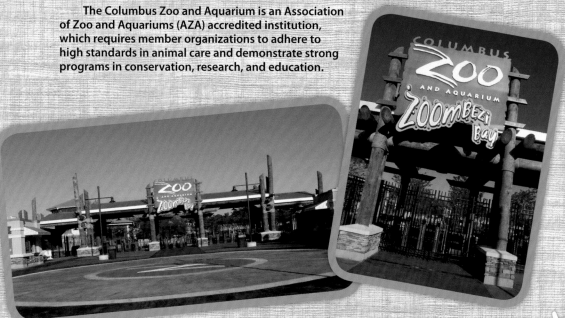

ABOUT THE AUTHOR

Nancy Roe Pimm volunteered as a docent for the Columbus Zoo and Aquarium in the 1980s. After she took an animal-handling class, the zoo entrusted her to go along with staff as they took critters to local school assemblies. Her favorites were Minnie and Max, the opossums. Another docent duty was to lead zoo tours. While giving the tours, Nancy discovered her fascination with the gorillas, especially Colo and her family. In 2007 Nancy's book, *The Heart of the Beast: Eight Great Gorilla Stories*, was published.

Born and raised in Brooklyn, New York, Nancy now resides in Plain City, Ohio, along with her husband, Ed, who has retired from racecar driving. They have three daughters: Allison, Lindsay, and Carli and a son-in-law, Rusty. Nancy is the proud grandmother of a grandson, Tommy.

Other books by the author include: *Indy 500: The Inside Track* and *Daytona 500: The Thrill and Thunder of the Great American Race*. Nancy still loves to visit schools, but instead of sharing animals, she shares her love of writing and reading and offers a message to the students to believe in their dreams.

Nancy Roe Pimm